AF428320

THE
Lucky Numbers
Dream Guide

Discovering Your Lucky Numbers

Dr. Jilesh

Copyright © 2023 by Jilesh Thilakan

All rights reserved. No part of this book may be reproduced, distributed, or transmitted in any form or by any means, including photocopying, recording, or other electronic or mechanical methods, without the prior written permission of the copyright holder, except in the case of brief quotations embodied in critical reviews and certain other non-commercial uses permitted by copyright law.
For permissions requests, write to the publisher at the address below:
Publisher: Jilesh Thilakan, India
Website: www.healingoraclewisdom.com[1]
Email: drjilesht@gmail.com
Cover design by Jilesh Thilakan

Disclaimer: The information provided in this book is for general informational purposes only. The content is based on the topic of lucky numbers and dream interpretation related to numbers. The interpretation of dreams and the notion of lucky numbers are subjective and can vary from person to person and culture to culture. The author and publisher disclaim any liability for any loss or damage incurred by the reader or any third party directly or indirectly as a result of the use or application of the information presented in this book.

The reader is encouraged to approach the content of this book with an open mind and use the knowledge for personal exploration and entertainment purposes only. This book is not intended as a substitute for professional advice or financial guidance.

---

1. http://www.healingoraclewisdom.com/

DR. JILESH

While the information in this book may provide insight into dream interpretation and lucky numbers, it is essential to remember that any decisions based on this information are the sole responsibility of the reader.

About the Author

Dr. Jilesh is a renowned and highly rated Manifestation Expert, Spell Caster, Psychotherapist, Life Coach, and Master of Business Administration. With extensive experience and expertise in the field, Dr. Jilesh has garnered a reputation as a trusted authority in the realm of manifestation and personal transformation.

As a highly rated manifestation expert and spell caster on Fiverr, Check Global Reviews here - https://www.fiverr.com/jileshthilakan?up_rollout=true[1] Dr.Jilesh has assisted countless individuals in manifesting their desires and achieving their goals. Through his deep understanding of the principles of manifestation, Dr. Jilesh has helped clients tap into their innate power to create their dream reality.

In addition to his work on Fiverr, **Dr. Jilesh has also excelled as a highly rated instructor on Udemy, with more than 30k students** Check his personal development courses here - https://www.udemy.com/user/jilesh-thilakan/ [2]sharing his knowledge and empowering students worldwide to harness the power of manifestation. With a passion for teaching and a commitment to providing valuable insights, Dr. Jilesh has garnered a loyal following of students who have experienced transformation and success under his guidance.

Dr. Jilesh's expertise extends beyond manifestation, as he is also a qualified psychotherapist and life coach. His background in psychology and counselling allows him to provide holistic support to individuals seeking personal growth and transformation. Through his empathetic approach and profound insights, Dr. Jilesh helps clients overcome challenges, break through limiting beliefs, and create lasting positive change in their lives.

Furthermore, Dr. Jilesh holds a master's degree in business administration, which adds a unique perspective to his work. His understanding of business principles and strategies allows him to guide individuals in aligning their personal goals with professional success, creating a harmonious balance between their aspirations and career pursuits.

With a diverse skill set and a genuine passion for helping others, Dr. Jilesh is committed to empowering individuals to unlock their full potential and manifest a life of abundance, fulfilment, and joy. Through his teachings, guidance, and transformative techniques, he aims to inspire and support others on their journey towards manifesting their deepest desires and living their best lives. For more about Author checkout his Blog- https://www.healingoraclewisdom.com/

---

1. https://www.fiverr.com/jileshthilakan?up_rollout=true

2. https://www.udemy.com/user/jilesh-thilakan/

Introduction

In the realm of dreams, where reality merges with the ethereal, lies a mysterious portal to the unknown - a pathway paved with symbols and enigmatic numbers that hold the key to unlocking the secrets of luck and fortune. Welcome to "The Lucky Numbers Dream Guide: Discovering Your Lucky Numbers," a captivating journey that will transport you into the mesmerizing world of dreams and numerology, where destiny intertwines with the whispering winds of chance.

Have you ever wondered if there is more to your dreams than mere fragments of imagination? Have you ever felt a profound connection to certain numbers, as if they held an invisible thread tying you to the grand tapestry of the universe? If so, you are about to embark on a voyage of self-discovery and revelation that will forever change the way you perceive the power of dreams and numbers in your life.

In this extraordinary guide, we invite you to unravel the enigma of dreams- those ephemeral visions that emerge from the depths of your subconscious mind. We will journey together through the annals of history, where ancient civilizations revered dreams as divine messages, and where the secrets of numerology were whispered among the wise.

Prepare to be captivated as we unveil the hidden messages and symbols that reside within your dreams. Each dream carries a unique code, an intricate tapestry of symbols carefully woven together to communicate truths that often elude our conscious awareness. We will teach you the language of dreams, a timeless lexicon that reveals the path to your deepest desires and wildest aspirations.

But this journey is not solely about dreams; it is also an exploration of the magical world of numerology. Numbers, those seemingly ordinary digits, possess extraordinary powers that shape the very fabric of our lives. From birthdates to license plates, numbers influence our decisions, our relationships, and even our destinies. Delve into the mystical art of numerology as we unravel the significance of each number archetype and discover your personal lucky numbers.

Throughout this book, we will empower you with practical tools and exercises to cultivate dream awareness, enhance dream recall, and even harness the power of lucid dreaming. With this newfound awareness, you will learn to navigate the labyrinth of your dreams, deciphering the cryptic messages that guide you

toward your lucky numbers and lead you to a life brimming with serendipity.

As you turn each page, you will become the architect of your own luck, embracing the wisdom of your dreams and numbers as a guiding force in your decisions and endeavours. With the art of manifestation, you will learn to shape your reality, attracting abundance and prosperity like a magnet draws iron.

But be forewarned - the path to discovering your lucky numbers is not merely a collection of techniques; it is an immersive journey of self-discovery, a process of unveiling the hidden facets of your innermost self. So, take a leap of faith into the unknown, for within these pages, your dreams will dance, and your numbers will sing the songs of your destiny.

Are you ready to venture into the mystical realm of dreams and numerology? If so, let us begin this extraordinary odyssey, for the Lucky Numbers Dream Guide awaits you, ready to unlock the secrets that will forever change the trajectory of your life. Let your dreams be your guide, and may the numbers lead you to the treasures that await on the shores of fortune.

Chapter 1
The Language of Dreams

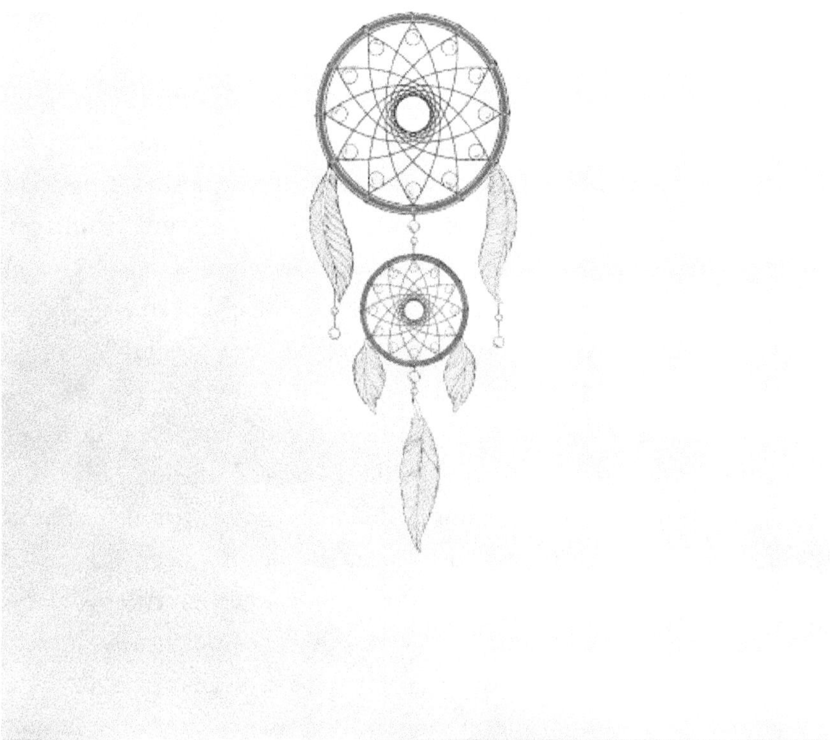

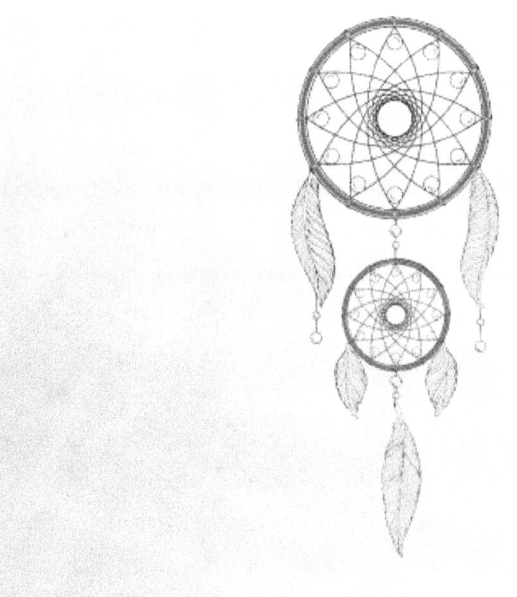

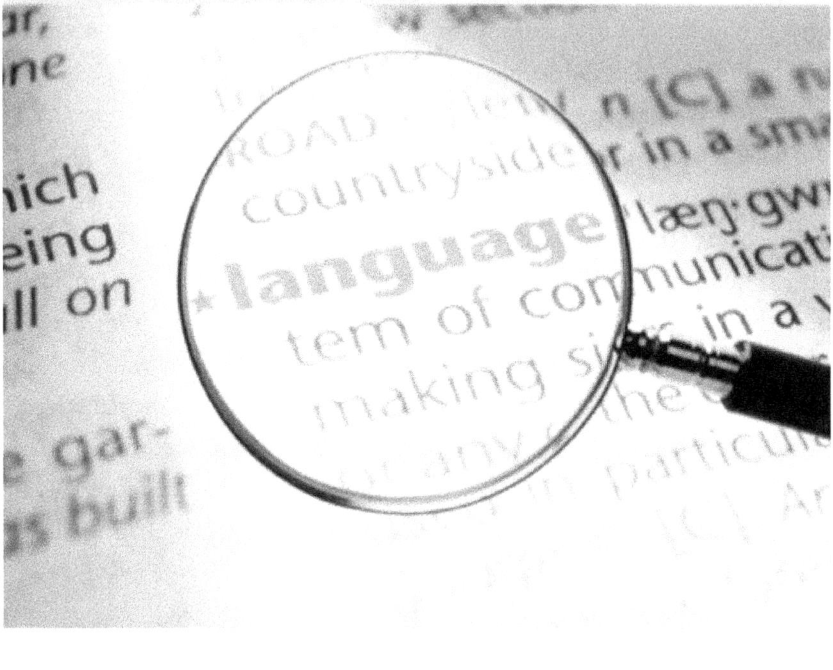
ar,
ne
ich
eing
ll on
e gar-
s built
ROAD
n [C]
countryside
r in a sma
language
tem of communicat
making si

In the silent realm of slumber, where reality fades into the background, dreams emerge as enigmatic narratives woven by the subconscious mind. They are the nocturnal symphonies of our deepest desires, fears, and aspirations, expressed through surreal landscapes and symbolic images. Welcome to Chapter 1 of "The Lucky Numbers Dream Guide: Discovering Your Lucky Numbers," where we embark on an exploration of the language of dreams and the profound messages they carry.

The Mystique of Dreams

Since the dawn of human civilization, dreams have captivated our collective imagination. Ancient cultures revered dreams as divine messages from the gods, guiding individuals and entire civilizations through cryptic symbols and visions. From the prophetic dreams of ancient Egypt to the healing dreams of Native American tribes, dreams were regarded as portals to higher realms of consciousness. Across cultures and throughout history, dreams have been perceived as a mysterious link between the mortal and the divine, providing insight into the unknown and unlocking the wisdom of the soul. Even today, psychologists and neuroscientists continue to study the profound implications of dreams, attempting to decode their language and unravel the secrets they hold.

The Many Facets of Dreams

Dreams are as diverse as the individuals who experience them. They can be delightful reveries, ominous premonitions, or profound journeys into the recesses of the mind. Some dreams may leave us with a sense of euphoria, while others linger as unsettling echoes in our waking thoughts. Recurring dreams, lucid dreams, and even nightmares each carry unique significance, reflecting various aspects of our subconscious minds. While the meanings of dreams may differ from one person to another, certain symbols and themes often recur, connecting us to universal archetypes and the collective unconscious.

Unravelling the Dream Symbols

At the heart of dream interpretation lies the art of unravelling dream symbols. Like ancient hieroglyphics etched upon the walls of the subconscious, symbols

in dreams carry potent meanings that may not always be immediately apparent. Understanding these symbols is akin to deciphering a secret code, a key to

unlocking the underlying messages within the dream. Common dream symbols include water, animals, flying, falling, and various elements of nature. Each symbol holds its unique resonance, representing emotions, experiences, or desires hidden beneath the surface of consciousness. For example, water often signifies emotions and the fluidity of life, while animals may represent instinctual drives or aspects of the self.

The Subconscious Mind's Playground

In dreams, the subconscious mind roams freely, liberated from the constraints of logic and time. This realm of the mind weaves together fragments of our waking experiences, memories, and emotions, creating narratives that may seem bizarre or nonsensical when juxtaposed against our waking reality. During sleep, the subconscious mind processes the events of the day, exploring unresolved conflicts and unspoken desires. Dreams offer a safe space for the subconscious to confront buried emotions and bring them to the forefront of our awareness. In this way, dreams serve as therapists of the mind, allowing us to gain insights and self-awareness that may elude us in our waking hours.

The Journey of Self-Discovery

Dreams can act as mirrors reflecting our innermost selves, illuminating facets of our personality and unresolved issues. Delving into dream analysis invites us on a journey of self-discovery, offering profound insights into our fears, hopes, and aspirations. By paying attention to recurring dreams or common symbols, we begin to unravel the threads of our subconscious patterns. Dreams provide us with valuable clues about the areas of our lives that require attention and nurturing. In essence, they are guideposts on our journey to self-improvement and personal growth.

The Influence of Culture and Beliefs

The interpretation of dreams is not only influenced by individual experiences but also by cultural and societal beliefs. Different cultures attribute diverse

meanings to dream symbols, reflecting their unique perspectives on life, spirituality, and the human psyche. For instance, a dream featuring a snake may be seen as a symbol of wisdom and transformation in some cultures, while in others, it may be associated with deceit and danger. Understanding the cultural nuances of dream symbolism allows us to appreciate the rich tapestry of human consciousness and its interpretation of dreams.

Tapping into the Collective Wisdom

Beyond individual dreams and cultural interpretations, the collective wisdom of humanity also plays a role in dream symbolism. Carl Jung, the renowned Swiss psychiatrist and psychoanalyst, introduced the concept of the collective unconscious - a repository of shared experiences and archetypal symbols that transcends cultural boundaries. Jung believed that certain dream symbols are part of this collective inheritance, reflecting universal themes and archetypes that are embedded in the human psyche. By tapping into this collective wisdom, we gain access to a deeper layer of meaning within our dreams, bridging the gap between the personal and the universal.

Dreamwork: Embracing the Enigma

Dreamwork is the art of engaging with and exploring dreams to gain deeper insights into our inner worlds. It involves various techniques such as dream journaling, guided meditations, and group discussions, all aimed at uncovering the hidden meanings within dreams. Through dreamwork, we learn to embrace the enigma of dreams, celebrating their mysteries rather than seeking definitive answers. Dream interpretation is not an exact science; rather, it is an intuitive dance with the subconscious, where each dreamer becomes both the artist and the canvas of their dreamscape.

The Journey Begins

As we venture further into "The Lucky Numbers Dream Guide: Discovering Your Lucky Numbers," let us remember that dreams are a kaleidoscope of the mind - a symphony of symbols and numbers waiting to be explored. They are the portals to self-awareness, offering us glimpses of our true potential and guiding us toward the fulfilment of our deepest desires. In the chapters that follow, we will delve deeper into the mysteries of dream symbolism and numerology. We will equip you with tools to interpret your dreams, recognize recurring symbols, and uncover the hidden messages they carry. Brace yourself for an extraordinary journey of self-discovery, where dreams and numbers converge to reveal the path to your destiny.

So, let us step into the realm of dreams, where the boundaries of reality blur, and the language of the soul finds its voice. For within the labyrinth of dreams lies the key to unlocking the secrets of luck and fortune, waiting to be discovered by the dreamer who dares to listen. As we set sail into this voyage of

the subconscious, may the whispers of dreams guide us to the treasures that await - the lucky numbers that will illuminate our paths and lead us to a life filled with serendipity and boundless possibilities. Let the adventure begin!

Chapter 2
The Power of Numerology

POWER

12 13 14
6 5
3
11 15
8
7
4
10
9 3 16
17 1 18
2
66 17

In the eternal dance of numbers, a profound language emerges, shaping the very fabric of our existence. Welcome to Chapter 2 of "The Lucky Numbers Dream Guide: Discovering Your Lucky Numbers," where we embark on an extraordinary journey into the mystical world of numerology. Within these digits lies the key to unlocking the secrets of our personalities, relationships, and destinies.

The Ancient Origins of Numerology

Numerology is an ancient practice that can be traced back to various civilizations, including the Babylonians, Egyptians, and Greeks. It is believed to have roots in both Eastern and Western cultures, with each region contributing unique insights into the power of numbers. The Pythagorean system of numerology, developed by the ancient Greek mathematician Pythagoras, is one of the most influential systems in Western numerology. Pythagoras saw numbers as the building blocks of the universe, with each number possessing a unique vibration and significance.

The Science and Art of Numerology

Numerology is a blend of science and art, combining the principles of mathematics with the intuitive interpretation of numbers' symbolism. It operates on the premise that every number has a specific energy that influences various aspects of our lives. The core belief in numerology is that our birth date and name carry vibrations that resonate with specific numbers. By decoding these vibrations, we gain insights into our personality traits, strengths, weaknesses, and even the timing of significant life events.

The Numerological Blueprint: Life Path Number

At the heart of numerology lies the Life Path Number, one of the most fundamental and influential numbers in a person's numerological blueprint. The Life Path Number is derived from the date of birth and reveals the path we are destined to walk in this lifetime. To calculate the Life Path Number, we reduce the birth date to a single digit, excluding the month and year. For example, if someone was born on October 15, 1985, the calculation would be: 1 + 0 + 1 + 5 + 1 + 9 + 8 + 5 = 30. Reducing further, 3 + 0 = 3. In this case, the Life Path Number is 3.

Each Life Path Number carries distinct qualities and characteristics. For

instance, a person with a Life Path Number 1 is a natural leader, innovative and ambitious, while someone with a Life Path Number 9 is compassionate, empathetic, and often drawn to humanitarian causes.

The Expression Number: Your True Self

The Expression Number, also known as the Destiny Number or the Talent Number, provides insights into our true selves - the abilities, talents, and potential that we possess. It is calculated from the full name at birth, reflecting the energies we project into the world. To determine the Expression Number, each letter in the full birth name is assigned a numerical value based on its position in the alphabet. For example, A=1, B=2, C=3, and so on. The values of all the letters are then added together and reduced to a single digit or a master number (11, 22, or 33). For instance, the Expression Number for the name "John Smith" would be calculated as follows: J=1, O=6, H=8, N=5, S=1, M=4, I=9, T=2, H=8. Adding all these values gives us 1 + 6 + 8 + 5 + 1 + 4 + 9 + 2 + 8 = 44. Since 44 is a master number, it is not reduced further. Therefore, the Expression Number for "John Smith" is 44. Each Expression Number signifies specific talents and attributes. A person with an Expression Number 7, for example, is introspective, analytical, and possesses a deep desire for knowledge and understanding. On the other hand, someone with an Expression Number 5 is adventurous, versatile, and seeks freedom and excitement.

The Soul Urge Number: Desires of the Heart

The Soul Urge Number, also known as the Heart's Desire Number, represents the deepest desires and innermost yearnings of a person's heart. It reveals the motivations that drive us and the things we crave on a soul level. To calculate the Soul Urge Number, we assign numerical values to the vowels in the full birth name and add them together, reducing to a single digit or a master number.

For example, in the name "Emma Johnson," the vowels are E=5, A=1, O=6, and O=6. Adding these values gives us 5 + 1 + 6 + 6 = 18. Reducing further, 1 + 8 = 9. Therefore, the Soul Urge Number for "Emma Johnson" is 9. Each Soul Urge Number corresponds to specific desires and aspirations. A person with a Soul Urge Number 2 seeks harmony and balance in relationships, valuing cooperation and connection. In contrast, someone with a Soul Urge Number 3 craves self-expression, creativity, and the joy of artistic pursuits.

The Personality Number: Outer Persona

The Personality Number, also known as the Outer Expression Number or the Minor Expression Number, reflects the persona we present to the outside world. It represents the first impression we make on others and how we navigate social interactions. To calculate the Personality Number, we assign numerical values to the consonants in the full birth name and add them together, reducing to a single digit or a master number. For instance, in the name "Michael Brown," the consonants are M=4, C=3, H=8, L=3, B=2, R=9, and W=5. Adding these values gives us $4 + 3 + 8 + 3 + 2 + 9 + 5 = 34$. Reducing further, $3 + 4 = 7$. Therefore, the Personality Number for "Michael Brown" is 7. Each Personality Number indicates specific traits and characteristics. A person with a Personality Number 1 exudes confidence, independence, and assertiveness. Conversely, someone with a Personality Number 6 appears nurturing, caring, and takes on a role of responsibility and service to others.

Master Numbers: The Power of 11, 22, and 33

In numerology, the numbers 11, 22, and 33 are known as master numbers and hold significant spiritual vibrations. These numbers are not reduced to a single digit as they carry a heightened level of potency and influence. The number 11 is associated with spiritual enlightenment, intuition, and divine inspiration. People with a prominent 11 in their numerological profile are often highly intuitive, visionary, and attuned to the mystical aspects of life. The number 22 is known as the Master Builder, representing the ability to turn dreams into reality. Those with a strong 22 influence possess remarkable organizational skills, ambition, and the capacity to manifest their aspirations into concrete achievements. Lastly, the number 33 is considered the Master Teacher, embodying the qualities of compassion, altruism, and selfless service. Individuals with a prominent 33 in their numerological chart often have a profound impact on the lives of others, guiding and inspiring them towards positive transformations.

Numerology and Your Birth Date

Numerology also places significance on the day, month, and year of your birth. By analysing the numbers present in your birth date, numerologists can gain deeper insights into your life's purpose and the lessons you are meant to learn in this lifetime. The Birth Day Number, calculated from the day of your birth, reveals your inherent strengths and weaknesses. It represents the gifts you were

born with and the challenges you may encounter on your life's journey. The Birth Month Number, calculated from the month of your birth, provides insights into your emotional nature and how you respond to various situations. Each month carries unique energies that influence your personality and life experiences. Lastly, the Year Number, calculated from the year of your birth, represents the overarching theme of a particular year in your life. This number can give you a sense of the opportunities and challenges that may arise during that time.

Timing and Personal Numerology

Numerology also involves understanding the cyclical nature of life and how numbers can be used to gain insights into specific periods and cycles. Personal Year Numbers and Personal Month Numbers are essential aspects of numerological timing. The Personal Year Number, calculated from your birth date and the current year, provides a sense of the overarching themes and energies that will influence your life during a particular year. It can help you align your actions and decisions with the prevailing energies of the year. The Personal Month Number, calculated from your Personal Year Number and the current month, offers a more specific focus on the opportunities and challenges you may encounter within a given month. Understanding your Personal Month Number can assist you in making the most of each month's potential.

Numerology and Relationships

Numerology's influence extends beyond individual readings; it also plays a significant role in understanding the dynamics of relationships. By examining the numerological profiles of two individuals, numerologists can assess the compatibility and challenges within a relationship. The Life Path Number is particularly crucial in relationship numerology. Compatible Life Path Numbers often indicate harmonious connections, shared values, and an innate understanding between partners. Conversely, incompatible Life Path Numbers may suggest potential conflicts and areas of tension in the relationship. Moreover, the Expression Numbers and Soul Urge Numbers of partners can also provide valuable insights into their compatibility. Understanding each person's desires, talents, and aspirations can help strengthen the relationship and foster mutual understanding and support.

The Transformative Power of Numerology

Numerology is more than a mere divinatory practice; it is a transformative tool that empowers individuals to embrace their true selves, align with their life's purpose, and make informed decisions. By delving into the world of numbers, we gain a deeper understanding of ourselves and our connection to the cosmos.

As we explore the profound influence of numerology on our lives, we are invited to recognize the patterns that emerge - signposts on our journey of self-discovery and personal growth. The power of numerology lies not only in predicting the future but in revealing the potential that lies dormant within us, waiting to be awakened.

Embracing Numerology: A Personal Voyage

Numerology beckons us to embark on a personal voyage, where numbers become our guiding stars, illuminating the path to self-awareness and fulfilment. By understanding the language of numbers, we gain a deeper appreciation for the intricacies of our being and our interconnectedness with the universe. As we continue our journey in "The Lucky Numbers Dream Guide: Discovering Your Lucky Numbers," let us open our hearts and minds to the transformative power of numerology. Let us embrace the wisdom that each number imparts, for within the realm of digits lies the key to unlocking our true potential and discovering the treasures of our destiny. The dance of numbers awaits us, where dreams and numerology intertwine to reveal the messages that have been whispering to us all along. With each number we uncover, we draw closer to the essence of our existence - a symphony of divine vibrations that guide us toward the fortunate shores of serendipity and abundance.

As we set sail into the vast ocean of numerology, may our journey be filled with wonder and enlightenment. For within the luminous tapestry of numbers, we find the answers to life's most profound questions and the wisdom to navigate the seas of uncertainty. Let us continue our quest to discover our lucky numbers, and may fortune smile upon us as we unlock the secrets of the universe - one digit at a time.

Chapter 3
Dreaming the Future: Prophetic Dreams

24

In the ethereal realm of dreams, time ceases to be linear, and visions of the past, present, and future intermingle in a tapestry of enigmatic symbols. Welcome to Chapter 3 of "The Lucky Numbers Dream Guide: Discovering Your Lucky Numbers." Here, we embark on a captivating exploration of prophetic dreams - the mysterious phenomenon of dreaming the future.

The Mystical Power of Prophetic Dreams

Since antiquity, humans have been intrigued by the notion of prophetic dreams - the idea that dreams can transcend the boundaries of time and space to offer glimpses of events yet to unfold. Prophetic dreams have been revered in cultures across the globe, from ancient civilizations to modern societies. These extraordinary dreams are believed to be portals through which the subconscious mind taps into the collective consciousness - a vast reservoir of knowledge that transcends individual experience. Prophetic dreams serve as a conduit between the mortal and the divine, offering profound insights into the unfolding of destiny.

Prophetic Dreams in History and Mythology

Throughout history, numerous accounts of prophetic dreams have been documented, enriching the tapestry of human experience. In ancient Greece, for instance, it was common for individuals to seek guidance from oracles, who often received their messages through prophetic dreams. One of the most famous examples of prophetic dreams can be found in the biblical story of Joseph. According to the Book of Genesis, Joseph had dreams that foretold his rise to power in Egypt, as well as the impending famine. These dreams played a pivotal role in the narrative of Joseph's life and demonstrated the significance of prophetic dreams in ancient times.

The Nature of Prophetic Dreams

Prophetic dreams can manifest in various forms, ranging from vivid, realistic visions to surreal and symbolic representations of future events.

They may offer glimpses of personal matters, such as life-changing decisions or encounters, as well as broader events with far-reaching consequences. While some prophetic dreams may be straightforward and easily interpreted, others require a deeper level of analysis and intuition to grasp their true meaning. The language of prophetic dreams is often layered with symbolism and allegory, demanding careful attention and interpretation.

The Role of Intuition in Prophetic Dreaming

Prophetic dreams are intricately connected to the intuitive faculties of the dreamer. Intuition acts as a bridge between the conscious and subconscious minds, allowing the dreamer to access higher realms of knowledge and perception. Cultivating and trusting one's intuition is vital in recognizing the prophetic elements within a dream. This innate inner knowing guides the dreamer to discern between ordinary dreams and those carrying prophetic messages, leading them to a deeper understanding of their significance.

Differentiating Prophetic Dreams from Ordinary Dreams

Distinguishing prophetic dreams from ordinary dreams can be a challenging task. Ordinary dreams often reflect the dreamer's daily experiences, emotions, and subconscious thoughts. On the other hand, prophetic dreams stand out as distinct and profound, transcending the usual boundaries of time and space.

Several key characteristics can help differentiate prophetic dreams from ordinary ones:

Clarity and Vividness: Prophetic dreams tend to be exceptionally vivid and clear, leaving a lasting impression on the dreamer's memory.

Specificity: Prophetic dreams often contain specific details and events that can be verified later.

Emotional Intensity: Prophetic dreams evoke powerful emotions and a sense of significance, leaving the dreamer with a lasting emotional impact.

Recurrence: Prophetic dreams may recur, presenting the same or similar visions multiple times to emphasize their importance.

Prophetic Déjà Vu: When the events depicted in a dream unfold in waking life, the dreamer may experience a sense of déjà vu, recalling the dream as it happens.

The Purpose of Prophetic Dreams

Prophetic dreams serve a myriad of purposes, offering guidance, warnings, and insights into the paths that lie ahead. They act as navigational beacons, steering the dreamer toward auspicious opportunities or deterring them from potential

pitfalls. In times of uncertainty or significant life decisions, prophetic dreams may provide valuable clarity and assurance, allowing the dreamer to make informed choices. They can also offer solace and comfort during challenging times, illuminating the path through adversity.

Prophetic Dreams and Personal Transformation

Experiencing a prophetic dream can be a transformative and life-altering event. These dreams challenge our conventional understanding of reality and the limitations of time, urging us to explore the depths of our consciousness and embrace the interconnectedness of all things. Prophetic dreams invite us to contemplate the nature of time and destiny, encouraging a more profound connection with our spiritual selves. As we delve into the mystery of these dreams, we awaken to the boundless potential of the human mind and the profound web of synchronicities that shape our lives.

Cultivating Prophetic Dream Awareness

While prophetic dreams are spontaneous occurrences, there are practices that can enhance dream recall and increase the likelihood of encountering prophetic dreams:

Dream Journaling: Keeping a dream journal is a powerful tool for enhancing dream recall and recognizing patterns in dreams, including prophetic elements.

Intent Setting: Before sleep, setting the intention to receive guidance or insights through dreams can invite prophetic experiences.

Meditation and Visualization: Engaging in meditation and visualization exercises can deepen one's connection to intuition and the subconscious mind.

Mindful Living: Practising mindfulness during waking hours can heighten awareness and lead to more vivid and memorable dream experiences.

Symbolic Interpretation: Developing the ability to interpret symbols in dreams can aid in recognizing prophetic elements within dream narratives.

The Ethics of Prophetic Dream Interpretation

When encountering prophetic dreams, ethical considerations come into play.

The interpretation of these dreams must be approached with sensitivity and respect for the dreamer's privacy and emotional well-being. Dreamers who experience prophetic dreams may seek guidance from trusted mentors, therapists, or spiritual counsellors to aid in understanding their significance. Open dialogue and empathy are essential when assisting dreamers in unravelling the messages contained within prophetic dreams.

The Paradox of Free Will and Destiny

The occurrence of prophetic dreams raises philosophical questions about the interplay between free will and destiny. While these dreams may offer glimpses of the future, the choices we make in waking life can influence the unfolding of events. Prophetic dreams present a paradox - a delicate dance between fate and choice, between what is predestined and what we have the power to shape. Embracing this paradox enriches our understanding of life's mysteries and the profound interconnectedness of all things.

Embracing the Mystery

As we delve into the realm of prophetic dreams, let us embrace the mystery that shrouds this fascinating phenomenon. Prophetic dreams serve as reminders of the limitless potential of the human spirit and the profound interconnectedness that binds us to the fabric of the universe.

May we approach each dream with reverence, curiosity, and an open heart, for within the realm of dreams lies the power to unveil the wonders of time and the treasures that await on the horizons of destiny. As we continue our exploration in "The Lucky Numbers Dream Guide: Discovering Your Lucky Numbers," let us remain attuned to the whispers of the future.

Chapter 4
The Lucky Number Archetypes

Lucky numbers

In the numerical symphony that shapes our lives, each number resonates with a unique vibration and significance. Welcome to Chapter 4 of "The Lucky Numbers Dream Guide: Discovering Your Lucky Numbers." Here, we explore the enchanting world of lucky number archetypes - the fundamental energies embodied by each number that influence our destinies.

Understanding Numerology Archetypes

Numerology archetypes are the foundational energies and characteristics associated with each number. These archetypes transcend cultural boundaries and hold universal significance, reflecting the essence of each number's vibrational frequency. Just as each instrument contributes a distinct melody to an orchestra, each number archetype imparts its unique qualities to the symphony of life. Understanding the lucky number archetypes empowers us to comprehend the hidden messages encoded within our birth dates and names.

The Number 1: The Pioneer

The number 1 embodies the archetype of the pioneer - the trailblazer who leads with courage, independence, and innovation. It is the number of new beginnings and individuality, symbolizing the power of self-expression and leadership.

Individuals influenced by the number 1 are driven, ambitious, and determined. They possess an innate ability to initiate change and make a significant impact on the world. The number 1 encourages us to embrace our uniqueness and step confidently onto the path of self-discovery.

The Number 2: The Peacemaker

The number 2 embodies the archetype of the peacemaker - the harmonizer who values cooperation, diplomacy, and compassion. It is the number of partnerships and relationships, symbolizing the importance of unity and balance. Individuals influenced by the number 2 are nurturing, empathetic, and adept at resolving conflicts. They have a natural affinity for collaboration and seek to create harmony in their personal and professional interactions. The number 2 encourages us to embrace the power of cooperation and the beauty of interdependence.

The Number 3: The Creative Visionary

The number 3 embodies the archetype of the creative visionary - the artist who

sees the world through a kaleidoscope of imagination and expression. It is the number of inspiration and joy, symbolizing the power of self-expression and creative manifestation. Individuals influenced by the number 3 are artistic, charismatic, and exude a zest for life. They possess a natural talent for communication and have a gift for bringing ideas to life. The number 3 encourages us to unleash our creativity and view the world as a canvas waiting to be adorned with our unique artistry.

The Number 4: The Solid Foundation

The number 4 embodies the archetype of the solid foundation - the builder who lays the groundwork for stability, order, and practicality. It is the number of structure and discipline, symbolizing the importance of hard work and determination. Individuals influenced by the number 4 are reliable, diligent, and committed to their goals. They possess a strong sense of responsibility and have a knack for organizing and strategising. The number 4 encourages us to embrace the virtues of diligence and create a strong foundation for our endeavours.

The Number 5: The Adventurer

The number 5 embodies the archetype of the adventurer - the free spirit who embraces change, curiosity, and exploration. It is the number of freedom and versatility, symbolizing the power of adaptability and embracing life's adventures. Individuals influenced by the number 5 are adventurous, curious, and open to new experiences. They have a natural inclination to explore and may find themselves drawn to diverse opportunities and lifestyles. The number 5 encourages us to embrace change, let go of limiting beliefs, and embrace the exhilarating journey of self-discovery.

The Number 6: The Nurturer

The number 6 embodies the archetype of the nurturer - the caregiver who embodies love, responsibility, and compassion. It is the number of family and community, symbolizing the importance of harmony and support. Individuals influenced by the number 6 are empathetic, compassionate, and devoted to the well-being of others. They have a natural affinity for creating nurturing environments and may excel in roles that require care and support. The number 6 encourages us to cultivate loving relationships and extend kindness and compassion to ourselves and those around us.

The Number 7: The Seeker of Truth

The number 7 embodies the archetype of the seeker of truth - the philosopher who delves into the mysteries of life and seeks inner wisdom. It is the number of spirituality and introspection, symbolizing the importance of inner growth and self-discovery. Individuals influenced by the number 7 are introspective, intuitive, and contemplative. They possess a deep desire to understand the underlying truths that govern existence. The number 7 encourages us to embark on a journey of self-exploration and to trust our intuition as we seek wisdom and enlightenment.

The Number 8: The Master Manifestor

The number 8 embodies the archetype of the master manifestor - the visionary who channels abundance, success, and material achievement. It is the number of prosperity and achievement, symbolizing the power of resilience and determination. Individuals influenced by the number 8 are ambitious, resourceful, and have a talent for turning dreams into reality. They possess a strong sense of purpose and are driven to succeed in their endeavours. The number 8 encourages us to harness our inner power and manifest our dreams with unwavering focus and determination.

The Number 9: The Humanitarian

The number 9 embodies the archetype of the humanitarian - the compassionate soul who dedicates themselves to serving humanity. It is the number of selflessness and altruism, symbolizing the importance of contributing to the greater good. Individuals influenced by the number 9 are empathetic, humanitarian, and driven by a sense of responsibility to make a positive impact on the world. They possess a deep understanding of the interconnectedness of all beings. The number 9 encourages us to embrace a spirit of service and contribute our unique gifts to create a better world for all.

Master Numbers and Their Significance

In addition to the single-digit numbers, master numbers 11, 22, and 33 hold profound significance in numerology. These numbers are considered master numbers because they carry a heightened level of spiritual vibration and potential. The number 11 is often associated with spiritual enlightenment and intuitive insight. Individuals influenced by the number 11 may possess psychic

abilities and a profound connection to higher realms of consciousness. The number 22 is known as the Master Builder, representing the ability to turn dreams into reality through practical application. Individuals influenced by the number 22 have the power to manifest their visions on a grand scale. The number 33 is considered the Master Teacher, embodying the qualities of compassion, altruism, and selfless service. Individuals influenced by the number 33 have a profound impact on the lives of others and are driven by a mission to uplift humanity. Master numbers carry immense spiritual potential, but their energy can also be intense and challenging to navigate. Those influenced by master numbers are called to embrace their higher calling and use their gifts to make a positive impact on the world.

Numerology and Personal Development

Understanding the lucky number archetypes can be a transformative tool for personal development and self-awareness. By exploring the significance of each number in our numerological profile, we gain insights into our strengths, weaknesses, and life's purpose. Numerology encourages us to embrace the diversity of our archetypal energies and leverage them to create a harmonious and fulfilling life. By aligning with the positive aspects of each archetype and working on the challenges they present, we embark on a journey of self-improvement and growth.

Numerology Archetypes and Relationships

Numerology archetypes also play a significant role in understanding the dynamics of relationships. By exploring the numerological profiles of two individuals, we can gain insights into the compatibility and challenges within the relationship. Compatible archetypes often indicate harmonious connections and shared values, while contrasting archetypes may suggest potential conflicts and areas of growth within the relationship.

Embracing the Diversity of Archetypal Energies

As we delve into the realm of numerology archetypes, let us embrace the diversity of energies that shape our lives. Each number archetype contributes a distinct melody to the symphony of our existence, and by understanding and embracing these energies, we become more attuned to our true selves.

May we find inspiration in the profound wisdom of numerology and the

archetypal energies that guide us on our journey of self-discovery and personal growth. As we continue our exploration in "The Lucky Numbers Dream Guide: Discovering Your Lucky Numbers," may we dance in harmony with the mystical symphony of numbers that holds the key to unlocking the treasures of our destiny.

Chapter 5
Cultivating Dream Awareness

DREAM

In the realm of dreams lies a vast landscape of symbolism, messages, and revelations waiting to be explored. Welcome to Chapter 5 of "The Lucky Numbers Dream Guide: Discovering Your Lucky Numbers." Here, we embark on a transformative journey of cultivating dream awareness - the art of delving deeper into our dreams and unlocking their hidden treasures.

The Mystique of Dreams

Dreams have captivated the human imagination for millennia, inspiring awe and wonder with their mysterious nature. From ancient civilizations to modern societies, dreams have been regarded as portals to other realms of consciousness - a realm where the boundaries between the waking and sleeping worlds blur. In our dreams, we encounter a myriad of experiences: surreal landscapes, familiar faces, symbolic encounters, and prophetic visions. Dreams hold a mirror to our innermost thoughts, emotions, and desires, providing profound insights into our psyche and soul.

The Importance of Dream Awareness

Dream awareness - the act of consciously engaging with our dreams - is a vital aspect of self-discovery and personal growth. By cultivating dream awareness, we open ourselves to a world of hidden wisdom and revelations that can positively impact our waking lives. When we pay attention to our dreams, we gain access to a wealth of untapped resources - our intuition, creativity, and higher consciousness. Dream awareness allows us to harness the transformative power of dreams, transforming them from mere nocturnal illusions into powerful tools for inner exploration.

The Dream Journal: A Pathway to Dream Awareness

The dream journal is a powerful tool for cultivating dream awareness. By recording our dreams upon waking, we bridge the gap between the dream realm and waking reality, preserving the essence of our nocturnal adventures. Keeping a dream journal helps us remember and make sense of our dreams. It allows us to recognize patterns, recurring symbols, and emotions within our dreams, facilitating deeper insights into our subconscious minds. To create a dream journal, keep a notebook or digital document by your bedside. As soon as you wake from a dream, jot down all the details you can remember - images, emotions, dialogue, and any other significant elements. Over time, you'll begin to notice themes and connections between your dreams, offering valuable

insights into your inner world.

Dream Interpretation: Unravelling the Symbols

Dreams often communicate through symbols, a language that speaks to the depths of our subconscious minds. Interpreting dream symbols is a creative and intuitive process, unique to each dreamer. When attempting to decipher dream symbols, consider the emotions and impressions they evoke within you. Reflect on personal associations with the symbols, as well as any cultural or archetypal meanings they may carry. Remember that dream symbols can have multiple layers of significance, reflecting different aspects of your life and psyche. Trust your intuition and embrace the unique meaning that emerges from your own exploration.

Lucid Dreaming: Awakening Within the Dream

Lucid dreaming is a state of heightened dream awareness - a state where the dreamer becomes conscious within the dream itself. In lucid dreams, we have the ability to recognize that we are dreaming and, in some cases, influence the dream's unfolding. Lucid dreaming opens up exciting possibilities for self-exploration and creative expression. By practising lucid dreaming techniques, we can consciously engage with our dreams, ask questions, and seek guidance from our inner wisdom. To enhance your chances of experiencing lucid dreams, incorporate reality checks into your waking life. Perform simple actions, such as looking at your hands or trying to read text, and question whether you are dreaming or awake. This habit will carry over into your dreams, triggering lucidity when you notice inconsistencies.

Dream Incubation: Inviting Specific Dreams

Dream incubation is the practice of setting intentions before sleep to invite specific dreams or seek guidance on particular issues. By consciously directing our dreams, we tap into the subconscious mind's problem-solving capabilities and creative potential. To practice dream incubation, take a few moments before sleep to focus on a specific question, problem, or topic. Write it down in your dream journal or repeat it as a mantra. Affirm your intention to receive guidance or insight in your dreams. Be patient and open to the ways in which the answer may manifest. Your dreams may offer direct responses, symbolic imagery, or subtle nudges that provide valuable insights and solutions.

Dream Recollection Techniques

Improving dream recall is essential for cultivating dream awareness. Dreams can quickly fade from memory upon waking, making it essential to capture their essence as soon as possible. Upon waking, lie still with your eyes closed, and try to recall the details of your dream. Gradually shift your focus from the external world to the dream world. Gently allow images and emotions to resurface, avoiding the urge to analyse or judge them. As you become more skilled at recalling dreams, you may find it helpful to recount your dreams out loud or record them in your dream journal immediately after waking.

Cultivating Mindfulness for Dream Awareness

Mindfulness practices are conducive to dream awareness, as they enhance our ability to stay present and attuned to our inner experiences. By cultivating mindfulness during waking hours, we carry this heightened awareness into the dream realm. Engage in mindfulness meditation to train your mind to observe thoughts, emotions, and sensations without judgment. This practice fosters a sense of clarity and presence, which can carry over into your dream awareness journey. Throughout the day, take moments to check in with your thoughts and emotions, anchoring yourself in the present moment. By building a foundation of mindfulness, you become more attuned to the subtle nuances of your dreams.

Dream Yoga and Spiritual Practice

In certain spiritual traditions, dream awareness is cultivated as a path to higher consciousness and spiritual awakening. Dream yoga, as practised in Tibetan Buddhism, is an advanced technique that involves working with dreams to recognize the illusory nature of reality and attain enlightenment. For practitioners of dream yoga, the dream state is seen as an opportunity for direct insight into the nature of the mind and its inherent clarity. Through lucid dreaming and other techniques, dream yogis explore the boundaries of consciousness and gain profound wisdom. While dream yoga is an advanced practice, all dreamers can draw inspiration from its principles. By recognizing the fluid nature of dreams and the potential for insight within them, we can deepen our connection to our higher selves and the spiritual dimensions of our lives.

Embracing the Magic of Dreams

As we journey deeper into the realm of dream awareness, let us embrace the magic and wonder of dreams. Dreams offer us a canvas for self-exploration, a portal to hidden realms of consciousness, and a gateway to profound insights.

May we approach our dreams with curiosity, reverence, and an open heart, for within the realm of dreams lie the keys to self-discovery, personal growth, and spiritual illumination. As we continue our exploration in "The Lucky Numbers Dream Guide: Discovering Your Lucky Numbers," may we awaken to the extraordinary power of dreams and unlock the treasures they hold for us - a symphony of enigmatic symbols and profound revelations that guide us on the path of destiny and self-realization.

Chapter 6
Interpreting Dream Symbols

46

Within the mystical tapestry of dreams, symbols are the threads that weave together the rich narratives of our subconscious minds. Welcome to Chapter 6 of "The Lucky Numbers Dream Guide: Discovering Your Lucky Numbers." Here, we embark on an illuminating journey of interpreting dream symbols - the art of deciphering the hidden meanings and messages concealed within our dreams.

The Language of Symbolism

Dreams communicate through a language of symbolism - a universal lexicon that transcends cultural and linguistic barriers. Symbols are the language of the subconscious, speaking in images, metaphors, and archetypal representations.

Just as an artist expresses emotions and ideas through brushstrokes on a canvas, our subconscious paints vivid pictures in our dreams. Interpreting dream symbols allows us to decipher the deeper meanings encoded in these images and gain profound insights into our inner worlds.

The Personal and Collective Unconscious

In dream analysis, we encounter both the personal unconscious and the collective unconscious. The personal unconscious comprises the unique experiences, memories, and emotions of the dreamer, while the collective unconscious is the reservoir of universal symbols and archetypes shared by all humanity. The collective unconscious, as proposed by Swiss psychologist Carl Jung, contains the "psychic inheritance" of the human species - a shared realm of symbols and themes that shape our dreams and cultural myths. When interpreting dream symbols, we must consider both the personal and collective significance of the symbols, as they often intertwine in meaningful and nuanced ways.

Archetypal Dream Symbols

Certain dream symbols carry universal significance and are considered archetypal in nature. These symbols emerge from the collective unconscious and hold consistent meanings across cultures and individuals.

Examples of archetypal dream symbols include:

The Shadow: Representing the hidden, repressed aspects of the self that the dreamer may be reluctant to confront.

The Hero: Symbolizing the dreamer's quest for self-discovery, growth, and transformation.

The Wise Old Man/Woman: Representing the dreamer's inner wisdom, guidance, and spiritual insight.

The Serpent: Often representing transformation, renewal, or even temptations and challenges.

The Crossroads: Symbolizing a significant decision or life choice that the dreamer must make.

Personal Dream Symbols

Alongside archetypal symbols, personal dream symbols are unique to the individual dreamer. These symbols emerge from the dreamer's personal experiences, memories, and emotional associations. Personal dream symbols can be objects, places, people, or even specific colours that hold particular significance to the dreamer. For example, a childhood toy may evoke feelings of nostalgia and comfort, while a particular location may symbolize a pivotal moment in the dreamer's life. When interpreting dream symbols, it is essential to consider both the universal and personal associations they carry, as this holistic approach offers a more comprehensive understanding of the dream's message.

Emotions and Dream Symbols

Emotions play a crucial role in dream interpretation, as they often guide us toward the heart of the dream's meaning. Paying attention to the emotions experienced during a dream can provide valuable clues about its significance.

Dreams that evoke fear, anxiety, or discomfort may point to unresolved issues or hidden fears in the dreamer's waking life. Conversely, dreams filled with joy, excitement, or love may reflect feelings of contentment or fulfilment. By exploring the emotional landscape of our dreams, we deepen our understanding of our inner desires, conflicts, and aspirations.

Dream Series and Recurring Symbols

Recurring symbols in dreams, known as dream series, are common occurrences that carry heightened significance. These symbols can reappear across multiple

dreams or over extended periods of time. Dream series often indicate that certain themes or aspects of the dreamer's life require attention and exploration. The repetition of symbols may serve as a signal from the subconscious, urging the dreamer to pay closer attention to certain aspects of their waking life or inner world. Recording dream series in a dream journal allows the dreamer to detect patterns and changes in the dream landscape over time, facilitating a more profound exploration of the dream's messages.

Cultural and Personal Context

Interpreting dream symbols requires an appreciation for cultural context and the dreamer's personal background. Cultural influences can shape the meaning of symbols, adding layers of significance that may not be immediately apparent. For example, a snake may represent wisdom and transformation in one culture, while it may symbolize danger and deceit in another. Similarly, colours may carry different associations in various cultural settings. Furthermore, the dreamer's personal experiences and associations with symbols can also influence their interpretation. An object that holds positive memories for one dreamer may trigger negative emotions in another, leading to distinct interpretations of the same symbol. Cultural and personal context adds depth and complexity to dream analysis, encouraging dreamers to explore the multi-faceted nature of symbols.

Common Dream Symbols and Their Meanings

While dream symbols can be highly individual, certain symbols recur frequently across different dreamers, cultures, and contexts. Here are some common dream symbols and their possible interpretations:

Water: Symbolizing emotions, subconscious feelings, and the flow of life.

Flying: Reflecting a sense of freedom, liberation, or a desire to rise above challenges.

Falling: Suggesting feelings of insecurity, loss of control, or fear of failure.

Doors: Representing opportunities, new beginnings, or transitions in life.

Vehicles: Symbolizing the direction and progress of the dreamer's journey through life.

Houses: Reflecting the dreamer's sense of self and the different aspects of their life.

Bridges: Indicating transitions or connections between different phases or states of being.

Animals: Representing various aspects of the dreamer's personality, instincts, or emotions.

Money: Reflecting the dreamer's sense of self-worth, abundance, or financial concerns.

Teeth: Suggesting issues related to communication, self-expression, or vulnerability.

It is essential to approach dream symbol interpretations with an open mind and a willingness to explore the unique meanings they hold for each dreamer.

Intuition and Dream Interpretation

In the realm of dream interpretation, intuition plays a vital role in unravelling the deeper meanings of symbols. Intuition guides us beyond the surface-level analysis of symbols, tapping into the wisdom of the subconscious mind. When interpreting dream symbols, trust your gut instincts and inner knowing. Avoid overanalysing or forcing interpretations, as this can lead to the dismissal of valuable insights from the intuitive realm.

Keeping a Symbol Dictionary

Maintaining a symbol dictionary can be a valuable resource for dream interpretation. This dictionary can include both universal and personal meanings of symbols, as well as any cultural associations that may apply. As you encounter various symbols in your dreams, add them to your dictionary along with your interpretations and feelings associated with them. Over time, this compilation becomes a personalized guide to your unique dream language.

Consulting Dream Experts and Therapists

For deeper exploration of dream symbols and their meanings, consider consulting dream experts or therapists who specialize in dream analysis. These

professionals can offer guidance and insights into the complex world of dream symbolism, enriching your understanding of your dreams and their messages.

Embracing the Enchantment of Dream Symbols

As we journey through the realm of dream symbolism, let us embrace the enchantment and mystery of dreams. Dream symbols serve as beacons of wisdom, guiding us on a path of self-discovery and personal growth.

May we approach dream interpretation with curiosity, reverence, and an open heart, for within the realm of dreams lie the keys to unlocking the hidden chambers of our subconscious minds. As we continue our exploration in "The Lucky Numbers Dream Guide: Discovering Your Lucky Numbers," may we dance with the symbolism that shapes our dreams and illuminates the path to self-realization and the treasures of destiny that await us.

Chapter 7
Dream Journaling for Luck

54

DREAM
JOURNAL

Within the depths of our dreams lies a reservoir of wisdom and insight that can lead us to a more fortunate and fulfilling life. Welcome to Chapter 7 of "The Lucky Numbers Dream Guide: Discovering Your Lucky Numbers." Here, we delve into the practice of dream journaling for luck - a transformative method for harnessing the power of dreams to manifest positive outcomes and unlock the secrets of good fortune.

The Power of Dream Journaling

Dream journaling is a sacred act of recording our nocturnal adventures, preserving the essence of our dreams upon waking. The act of journaling offers a tangible connection to the dream realm, allowing us to explore the hidden messages and symbolism woven within our dreams. Beyond mere documentation, dream journaling serves as a bridge between the conscious and subconscious minds. As we recount our dreams on paper, we invite our waking awareness to interact with the enigmatic realm of dreams, enabling us to uncover valuable insights and harness the power of our dreams for luck and manifestation.

Setting Intentions for Luck

The journey of dream journaling for luck begins with setting clear intentions before sleep. By directing our focus and energy toward inviting fortunate and serendipitous dreams, we pave the way for the subconscious to work its magic.

Before bedtime, take a few moments to set your intention for luck and positive outcomes. State your intention aloud or write it in your dream journal, affirming your desire to receive guidance and insights that lead to fortunate events in your waking life. As you embark on this practice, maintain an open mind and a heart receptive to the signs and symbols that may unfold in your dreams.

Capturing Fortunate Dreams

As you awaken from your dreams, gently retrieve the essence of your dreamscapes and record them in your dream journal. Pay attention to any themes, symbols, or emotions that stand out, as these may hold the keys to unlocking the secrets of luck and manifestation.

Consider the following elements as you journal your dreams:

Symbols: Reflect on any symbols or recurring images that appear in your dreams. These symbols may carry deeper meanings and insights into the fortunate events that await you.

Emotions: Take note of the emotions you experienced during the dream. Positive emotions, such as joy, excitement, or empowerment, may indicate auspicious opportunities.

Colours: Consider any significant colours that appeared in your dream. Colours can convey specific energies and messages related to luck and manifestation.

People: Reflect on the presence of specific individuals in your dream. People in dreams may represent aspects of yourself or hold symbolic significance related to luck.

Locations: Examine the settings and locations in your dreams. Certain places may hold personal or cultural associations with luck and positive outcomes.

Events and Actions: Pay attention to any events or actions that transpired in your dream. These actions may provide clues to actions you can take in your waking life to attract luck.

Recognizing Lucky Omens

Dreams often contain omens and signs that point toward fortunate events. As you journal your dreams, be attuned to these subtle messages, which can guide you toward favourable opportunities and serendipitous encounters.

Lucky omens in dreams can take various forms, such as:

Finding money or valuable items: Symbolizing abundance and financial luck.

Encountering symbols of good luck: Such as four-leaf clovers, horseshoes, or shooting stars.

Meeting wise and helpful mentors: Representing guidance and support on your path to luck.

Receiving gifts or rewards: Signifying recognition and positive outcomes.

Witnessing positive transformations: Indicating personal growth and favourable changes.

Dream Affirmations for Luck

Incorporating dream affirmations into your practice can amplify the power of dream journaling for luck. Dream affirmations are positive statements that you repeat before sleep to program your subconscious mind for fortunate dreams and manifestations.

Craft affirmations that align with your intentions for luck and abundance. For example:

"I attract good fortune and serendipitous opportunities into my life."

"I am open to receiving positive guidance and insights in my dreams."

"My dreams lead me to fortunate encounters and favourable outcomes."

"Every dream I record in my journal brings me closer to my desired manifestations."

Recite your chosen affirmation several times before sleep, allowing its positive energy to infuse your subconscious mind.

Dream Incubation for Luck

Dream incubation is a powerful technique that involves directing your dreams toward specific themes or desired outcomes. To harness the power of dream incubation for luck, focus on inviting dreams that offer insights and guidance related to fortunate events and opportunities. Before sleep, meditate on your intention for luck and good fortune. Visualize the scenarios and outcomes you desire in your waking life. Create a mental image of yourself experiencing positive and auspicious events. As you drift into slumber, repeat your dream incubation intention, inviting your subconscious mind to unfold dreams that lead you closer to your desired manifestations.

Dream Alchemy: Transforming Night into Day

Dream alchemy is the process of translating dream insights and symbols into actionable steps in your waking life. As you journal your dreams, consider how the wisdom gleaned from the dream realm can guide you to create luck and manifestation in your daily experiences.

Ask yourself:

What messages or insights from my dream can I apply to my current challenges or aspirations?

How can I integrate the emotions and symbols from my dream to attract positive outcomes in my waking life?

Are there any actions or decisions I can take inspired by my dream to invite luck and abundance?

Dream alchemy bridges the gap between the dream realm and waking reality, empowering you to utilize the wisdom of your dreams to create a more fortunate and fulfilling life.

Dream Visualization for Luck

In addition to dream journaling, dream visualization is a potent tool for manifesting luck and positive outcomes. As you prepare for sleep, engage in a visualization practice that aligns with your intentions for luck. Close your eyes and imagine yourself experiencing fortunate events, encountering positive opportunities, and attracting abundance in your life. Engage all your senses in this visualization - see the scenes vividly, feel the emotions of joy and gratitude, and embrace the sensations of luck and fulfilment. Immerse yourself in the dream-like realm of your visualization, knowing that the power of your subconscious mind is receptive to these positive imprints. Trust that your dreams will respond to the energy you invest in this practice.

Cultivating Gratitude for Dream Luck

Gratitude is a potent force for attracting more luck and abundance into our lives. As you journal your dreams and engage in dream visualization, cultivate gratitude for the insights and guidance you receive from the dream realm.

Express gratitude for each fortunate dream you experience, regardless of its significance or size. The act of acknowledging and appreciating these fortunate dreams sets the stage for more luck to flow into your life.

Integrating Dream Luck into Daily Life

Dream journaling for luck is not a stand-alone practice; it is a pathway to aligning your dreams with your waking reality. As you continue this transformative journey, seek opportunities to integrate the wisdom and insights gained from your dreams into your daily life. Take actionable steps inspired by your dreams, and be open to following the guidance and signs they offer. Trust that the fortunate events unfolding in your dreams hold the potential to manifest in your waking life when you embrace the magic of synchronicity and serendipity.

A Tapestry of Fortune Unfolds

As you embark on the practice of dream journaling for luck, remember that the tapestry of fortune is woven from the threads of your intentions, dreams, and actions.

May you embrace the enchantment of dreams and cultivate the art of dream journaling for luck. As you continue your exploration in "The Lucky Numbers Dream Guide: Discovering Your Lucky Numbers," may you unlock the secrets of your destiny and navigate the currents of fortune with grace and serendipity.

Chapter 8

The Enchanting World of Lucky Numbers - Utilization for Prosperity and Abundance

Throughout human history, the allure of lucky numbers has captivated people from diverse cultures and belief systems. These numbers, often regarded as symbols of good fortune and prosperity, hold a universal appeal, transcending boundaries and time. In this chapter, we will explore the enchanting world of lucky numbers, diving into their symbolism, cultural significance, and the ways they can be harnessed to attract prosperity and abundance.

Understanding the Power of Lucky Numbers

Defining Lucky Numbers

Lucky numbers are those imbued with positive attributes and believed to bring good luck to those who encounter or incorporate them into their lives. These numbers hold various symbolic meanings, often representing elements like success, abundance, spiritual enlightenment, and harmonious relationships.

The Timeless Fascination with Lucky Numbers

The fascination with lucky numbers is deeply rooted in human history. Ancient civilizations, such as the Chinese, Indians, Greeks, and Egyptians, recognized the potential of numbers to influence life events and sought to understand their significance in mystical contexts. This enduring intrigue continues to shape cultural practices and personal beliefs to this day.

Cultural Significance of Lucky Numbers

China - The Power of Eight

In Chinese culture, the number eight holds exceptional significance. Its phonetic similarity to the word for "prosperity" makes it an auspicious number associated with wealth and success. The number eight is often favoured in business deals, weddings, and important events to attract prosperity and good fortune.

India - The Sacred Nine

In India, the number nine is considered sacred and powerful. Associated with the Navagraha, the nine celestial deities governing planetary influences, it represents completeness and spiritual attainment. The Navaratri festival, celebrated over nine nights, honours these celestial entities.

Western Numerology

Western numerology ascribes meanings to numbers, linking them to various attributes and energies. For instance, the number seven is often connected to wisdom and introspection, while the number three is associated with creativity and self-expression. Individuals who encounter these numbers may perceive them as symbols of encouragement or guidance.

Embracing a Pantheon of Lucky Numbers

Number One - Unity and New Beginnings

The number one symbolizes unity, individuality, and fresh starts. In Chinese culture, it represents leadership and ambition. For those seeking personal growth and advancement, the number one holds significance.

Number Two - Balance and Harmony

The number two signifies balance, harmony, and cooperation. It is associated with partnerships and is often considered lucky in matters of love and marriage.

Number Three - Creativity and Harmony

Lucky number three is linked to creativity, harmony, and fulfilment of desires. Many cultures believe that good things come in threes, making this number an auspicious symbol for a variety of endeavours.

Number Four - Prosperity and Growth

The number four is associated with prosperity and growth. In Chinese culture, it represents double prosperity, making it an auspicious number for business ventures and financial success.

Number Six - Happiness and Prosperity

The number six symbolizes happiness and prosperity. In various cultures, it is believed to promote smooth progress and harmonious relationships, making it auspicious for family and community-related matters.

Number Seven - Divine Perfection

Lucky number seven is associated with divine perfection and completeness. It is revered in numerous cultures and belief systems for its positive qualities.

Number Eight - Abundance and Wealth

As previously mentioned, the number eight is highly regarded for its connection to abundance and wealth. Its phonetic resemblance to the word for "prosperity" cements its reputation as an auspicious number for financial success.

Number Nine - Spiritual Enlightenment

Number nine holds spiritual significance, representing completeness and spiritual enlightenment. It is associated with wisdom and the pursuit of spiritual growth.

Number Eleven - Awakening and Intuition

The number eleven is considered a master number, symbolizing spiritual awakening and intuition. Individuals associated with this number are often seen as spiritually gifted and destined for higher purposes.

Number Fourteen - Double Prosperity

The number fourteen is believed to bring double prosperity. It is associated with success and favourable outcomes, especially in business ventures.

Number Twenty-One - Success and Victory

Number twenty-one is linked to success and victory. In card games and gambling, this number often represents winning hands.

Number Twenty-Two - Master Builder

The number twenty-two is a master number, known as the "Master Builder." It signifies the ability to turn dreams into reality and make significant contributions to society.

Number Thirty-Three - The Master Healer

Similar to number eleven, thirty-three is a master number representing the "Master Healer." It embodies compassion and the capacity to uplift others.

Number Forty-Two - Universal Understanding

Forty-two is associated with universal understanding and the pursuit of knowledge. It is a number that provides insights into the deeper meaning of life and existence.

Number Forty-Nine - Divine Protection

Number forty-nine is considered a powerful and protective number, believed to offer divine blessings and guard against negativity.

Number Fifty - Abundance and Fulfilment

The number fifty is associated with abundance and fulfilment. It represents material and spiritual prosperity.

Number Sixty-Six - Family and Home

Number sixty-six symbolizes family, home, and nurturing. It is considered fortunate for matters related to family life and harmony.

Utilizing Lucky Numbers for Prosperity and Abundance

Dream Journaling

Keeping a dream journal can help individuals identify patterns and recurring lucky numbers that appear in their dreams. By understanding the context in which these numbers manifest, one can gain insights into subconscious desires and aspirations.

Numerology Consultations

Consulting with a numerologist provides a deeper analysis of lucky numbers and their significance. These experts interpret the numbers in various contexts and offer guidance on utilizing them to attract prosperity and abundance.

Visualization and Affirmations

Incorporating lucky numbers into daily visualization and affirmation practices can align the mind with positive energy and intentions. Visualizing oneself surrounded by abundance while focusing on lucky numbers can enhance the attraction of favourable outcomes.

Talismans and Amulets

Wearing or carrying talismans and amulets inscribed with lucky numbers provides a constant reminder of one's aspirations and goals. These symbols are believed to draw positive energy and blessings into one's life.

Embracing Positive Change

Harnessing lucky numbers is not solely about relying on luck but also about adopting a positive mindset and embracing change to invite prosperity and abundance. Taking proactive steps towards personal and financial growth, coupled with belief and action, contribute to achieving positive outcomes.

The enchanting world of lucky numbers encompasses a rich tapestry of symbolism, cultural beliefs, and personal interpretations. From the auspiciousness of number eight to the spiritual enlightenment represented by number nine and the masterful manifestations of numbers eleven and twenty-two, each number carries its own unique allure. Embracing these lucky numbers in various aspects of life is a testament to the timeless human desire for hope, optimism, and a touch of magic as we navigate the journey towards prosperity and abundance. Whether we turn to cultural traditions, numerology, or personal experiences, the allure of lucky numbers continues to inspire us to seek out positive outcomes and embrace the potential for growth and success in every facet of life.

Chapter 9
Integrating Luck into Your Daily Life

live
your
dream.

luck

The pursuit of luck is not merely a quest for fleeting moments of chance; it is a way of being - a conscious choice to align with the energies of good fortune and serendipity. Welcome to Chapter 9 of "The Lucky Numbers Dream Guide: Discovering Your Lucky Numbers." Here, we embark on a transformative journey of integrating luck into your daily life - a practice that invites the magic of synchronicity and abundance into every aspect of your existence.

Embracing the Mindset of Luck

Luck begins with a mindset - a belief in the inherent potential for positive outcomes and fortunate events. Embrace the mindset of luck by shifting your perspective to see opportunities in challenges and silver linings in every situation. Cultivate an attitude of gratitude for the blessings and abundance in your life, recognizing that an attitude of appreciation magnetizes more luck and positivity.

Embodying Optimism and Positivity

Optimism and positivity are powerful magnets for luck and serendipity. Embody these qualities by consciously choosing positive thoughts, language, and actions. Practice affirmations that reflect your belief in good fortune and repeat them daily. Surround yourself with positive influences, inspiring books, and uplifting media that nurture your optimistic outlook.

Embracing Change and Adaptability

Embracing change and cultivating adaptability are key traits of lucky individuals. Embrace the fluidity of life, and be open to new experiences and opportunities that come your way. Fearlessly step outside your comfort zone and explore uncharted territories. Embracing change allows you to seize fortunate opportunities and create luck in unexpected ways.

Cultivating Resilience and Perseverance

Resilience and perseverance are pillars of a fortunate life. Understand that setbacks and challenges are part of the journey.

Cultivate resilience by bouncing back from adversity with grace and determination. Keep moving forward with unwavering perseverance, even in the face of obstacles. Resilience and perseverance pave the way for fortuitous outcomes.

Taking Inspired Action

Luck favours those who take inspired action. Be proactive and seize opportunities as they arise. Act on your dreams, goals, and intuitions with a sense of purpose and determination. Remember that taking inspired action is not about forcing outcomes but aligning with the flow of life. Trust that the universe will respond to your actions with synchronicity and serendipity.

Listening to Intuition and Inner Guidance

Intuition is a profound guiding force that leads us to fortunate paths. Listen to your inner voice and follow the subtle nudges of your intuition. Create space for stillness and reflection, allowing your inner wisdom to speak to you. Embrace meditation, journaling, or any practice that fosters a connection with your intuition.

Surrounding Yourself with Positive Energy

The energy we surround ourselves with significantly impacts our luck. Surround yourself with positive and supportive individuals who uplift and inspire you. Create a positive environment in your home and workspace, infusing it with symbols of luck and abundance. Keep your surroundings clutter-free and harmonious, allowing positive energy to flow freely.

Practising Random Acts of Kindness

Random acts of kindness are a powerful way to invite luck into your life. Engage in selfless acts of generosity and compassion toward others. When you spread kindness, you create a ripple effect of positive energy that attracts fortunate experiences and people into your life.

Trusting the Power of Gratitude

Gratitude is the alchemy that transforms everyday moments into lucky blessings. Cultivate a daily gratitude practice, acknowledging and appreciating the abundance in your life. Express gratitude for fortunate events, serendipitous encounters, and even challenges that lead to growth and learning. Trust that the more you express gratitude, the more luck and abundance you will attract.

Creating Luck-Friendly Rituals

Rituals have the power to anchor luck into your daily life. Create luck-friendly rituals that align with your intentions for good fortune. Start your day with a positive affirmation or meditation for luck. Carry a lucky charm or talisman that holds special significance for you. Conclude your day with a gratitude ritual, reflecting on the fortunate events of the day.

Connecting with Nature

Nature is a wellspring of luck and inspiration. Spend time outdoors, connect with the natural world, and attune yourself to its rhythms. Nature rejuvenates the soul and helps you align with the flow of life, where luck and abundance thrive.

Embracing Serendipity

Serendipity is the delightful surprise of unexpected fortune. Embrace serendipitous moments with joy and wonder. Be open to the unexpected gifts and encounters that come your way, and trust that the universe has a way of weaving fortunate events into your life's tapestry.

Letting Go of Limiting Beliefs

Limiting beliefs can hinder the flow of luck and abundance. Let go of beliefs that no longer serve you and replace them with empowering beliefs. Believe in your worthiness to receive good fortune and trust that the universe is conspiring to bring positive outcomes your way.

Journaling for Luck and Abundance

Incorporate journaling for luck and abundance into your daily routine. Write down your intentions for fortunate outcomes, record serendipitous events, and express gratitude for the luck that unfolds in your life. Journaling provides a record of your luck journey and reinforces your positive mindset.

Visualizing Your Lucky Future

Engage in visualization practices that depict your life filled with luck and abundance. Visualize fortunate events, serendipitous encounters, and a life of fulfilment and joy. Immerse yourself in the emotions of living a lucky life, knowing that visualization is a powerful tool for manifestation.

Sharing Your Luck with Others

Luck multiplies when shared. Share your good fortune and abundance with others, whether through acts of kindness, mentorship, or charitable giving.

By sharing your luck, you create a virtuous cycle of positive energy that enriches the lives of those around you.

Trusting Divine Timing

Trust that the universe has perfect timing for every fortunate event. Release the need for immediate results and allow the process of luck to unfold naturally.

Have faith that the right opportunities will present themselves when the time is right.

Celebrating Your Luck Journey

Celebrate the fortunate events, synchronicities, and abundance in your life. Embrace a sense of joy and celebration for the luck that graces your path.

Celebrate not only the grand moments but also the small blessings that make life extraordinary.

Living a Life of Gratitude and Luck

The integration of luck into your daily life is an ongoing journey. Embrace a life of gratitude and luck, knowing that the more you cultivate these energies, the more they will grace your life.

As we conclude this chapter in "The Lucky Numbers Dream Guide: Discovering Your Lucky Numbers," may you carry the essence of luck into every moment, infusing your existence with serendipity and abundance. Embrace the magic of luck and open yourself to a world of fortuitous opportunities and joyful surprises. Trust that as you align with the energies of luck, the universe conspires to create a life of extraordinary possibilities.

Conclusion

Congratulations! You have reached the final page of "The Lucky Numbers Dream Guide: Discovering Your Lucky Numbers." Throughout this transformative journey, we have delved into the mystical realm of dreams, unlocked the secrets of numerology, and harnessed the power of luck and manifestation. As we conclude this adventure, I invite you to take a moment to reflect on the profound insights you have gained and the potential for transformation that lies before you.

In the pages of this book, you have discovered the language of dreams and the wisdom they hold. You have explored the mysteries of numerology and its profound impact on our lives. You have embraced dream awareness, interpreting dream symbols, and journaling for luck. Together, we have danced in harmony with the symphony of numbers, uncovering the enigmatic secrets of destiny and self-realization.

Now, armed with the knowledge and practices shared in this guide, you have the tools to manifest a life of luck, serendipity, and abundance. The path to luck is not one of blind chance but a conscious choice - a choice to embody the mindset of luck, align with the energies of good fortune, and embrace the magic of synchronicity.

As you continue your journey beyond these pages, remember that luck is not an external force but a reflection of your inner state of being. Cultivate a mindset of optimism, gratitude, and resilience. Trust in the power of your dreams, intuition, and synchronicities.

Each day offers a canvas on which to paint your fortune. Embrace the power of dream journaling, visualization, and positive action to create a life of meaning, purpose, and abundance. As you integrate the wisdom of this book into your daily life, may you step into the flow of destiny and welcome the fortunate events that await you.

I encourage you to share your luck journey with others and spread the magic of good fortune. As you embrace the wonders of your destiny, invite your friends, family, and fellow dreamers to embark on their own quests for luck and serendipity.

Finally, I would be incredibly grateful if you could take a moment to share your thoughts and experiences with "The Lucky Numbers Dream Guide: Discovering Your Lucky Numbers." Your reviews and feedback not only inspire

me but also guide others on their paths to luck and manifestation.

I believe in the transformative power of dreams and the magic of synchronicity. Together, we can create a world where luck and abundance grace every heart and soul. Thank you for joining me on this captivating journey. May your dreams be filled with serendipitous encounters, your heart be open to the wonders of the universe, and your life be a tapestry woven with the threads of luck and destiny.

With gratitude and anticipation,

Dr.Jilesh

www.ingramcontent.com/pod-product-compliance
Lightning Source LLC
Chambersburg PA
CBHW050600160726

48003CB00002B/979